GOOD HOUSEKEEPING HOUSEHOLD RECORD BOOK

EBURY PRESS STATIONERY

First published in 1991 by Ebury Press Stationery
An imprint of the Random Century Group
Random Century House, 20 Vauxhall Bridge Road,
London SW1V 2SA

Set in Horley Old Style
by FMT Graphics Limited, Southwark, London

Printed and bound in Hong Kong

Designed by Paul Welti
Text by Elizabeth Martyn

ISBN 0 7126 4556 X

Colour illustrations throughout this book have been taken from the front covers of Good Housekeeping *magazines published in the 1930's.*

CONTENTS

Introduction

This book will save you hours of time and irritation. With it you can forget about all those phone numbers scribbled on odd bits of paper, when and which of your children had measles and what time the last bus gets in.

Provided you fill in the data suggested on the following pages you will have all the information you need to run your daily life smoothly. You can remind yourself quickly about things that need doing, check how much wallpaper the bathroom took last time around and keep an eye on your household finances.

Take time and trouble to fill in all the relevant pages and to update them when necessary. Most of the information you put in will be a once-only record and it will be there for ever, easy to look up and easy to use.

Keep the Record Book by the telephone, on the kitchen shelf or somewhere else that's handy and train the rest of your household in how to use it. After all, you may not be available when someone needs a dentist or a takeaway in a hurry!

Cassandra Kent
GOOD HOUSEKEEPING

EMERGENCY!

EMERGENCY!

Make sure everyone in the family knows where to find this information in an emergency. Don't wait until disaster strikes: ensure that everyone knows how to escape from all floors of the house if there is a fire. At least one person in the family should have basic knowledge of first-aid.

IN THE EVENT OF FIRE, DIAL EMERGENCY SERVICES IMMEDIATELY AND GET EVERYONE OUT OF THE HOUSE. *DO NOT* ATTEMPT TO DEAL WITH A FIRE YOURSELF, UNLESS IT IS VERY SMALL.

EMERGENCY PHONE NOS

DOCTOR . . . .

First-aid kit is kept: . . . .

VET . . . .

LOCAL POLICE STATION . . . .

GAS BOARD (emergency number) . . . .
If you suspect a gas leak, do not light matches or operate any electrical appliances, including light switches. Open all windows.

ELECTRICITY BOARD (emergency number) . . . .

ELECTRICIAN . . . .

To turn off mains supply: . . . .

. . . .

WATER BOARD (emergency number) . . . .

PLUMBER . . . .

Note position of stopcocks . . . .

. . . .

EMERGENCY PHONE NOS

ADULTS' DAYTIME PHONE NOS ....

....

....

....

....

....

....

....

NEIGHBOURS/FRIENDS FOR CHILDREN TO CONTACT IN EMERGENCY ....

....

....

....

....

....

....

....

....

....

....

....

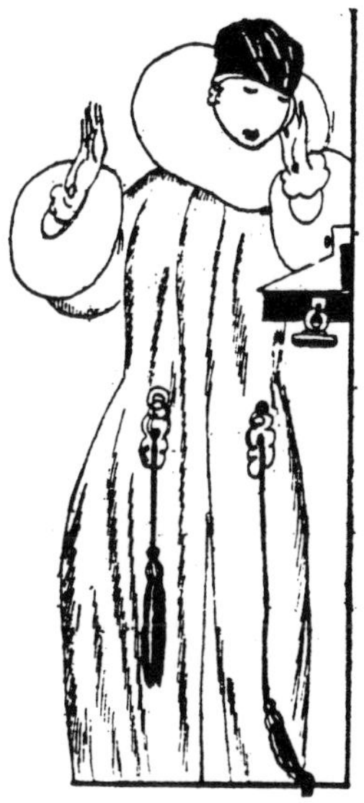

Emergency Phone Nos

Other emergency nos ....

....

....

....

....

....

....

....

....

....

....

....

....

....

....

....

....

....

....

....

LOCAL LIFE

DOMESTIC SERVICES

Use this page to record details of all the people and services you need to keep the household running smoothly. Add notes of availability, hours worked etc, where necessary.

BABYSITTER/S ....

....

....

CLEANER ....

GARDENER ....

ODD JOB/HANDYMAN ....

RUBBISH TIP (address and opening hours) ....

....

DELIVERY SERVICES (nappies, laundry, etc) ....

....

....

NEWSAGENT (phone no, details of order) ....

....

MILKMAN (phone no of dairy, details of order) ....

....

HIRE SHOP ....

OTHER DOMESTIC SERVICES ....

....

Personal Services

Hairdresser . . . .

Barber . . . .

Beauty salon . . . .

Manicurist . . . .

Chiropodist . . . .

Accountant . . . .

. . . .

Solicitor/Lawyer . . . .

. . . .

Bank Manager . . . .

. . . .

Financial Advisor . . . .

. . . .

Insurance Broker . . . .

. . . .

Stockbroker . . . .

. . . .

Other personal services . . . .

. . . .

. . . .

TRANSPORT

TAXI RANK/MINI-CAB ....

CAR HIRE ....

LOCAL RAIL STATION ....

Useful train times ....

LOCAL BUS STATION ....

Useful bus times ....

....

MAIN STATIONS: ENQUIRY NOS ....

....

....

AIRPORT: FLIGHT ENQUIRY NO ....

....

....

....

....

....

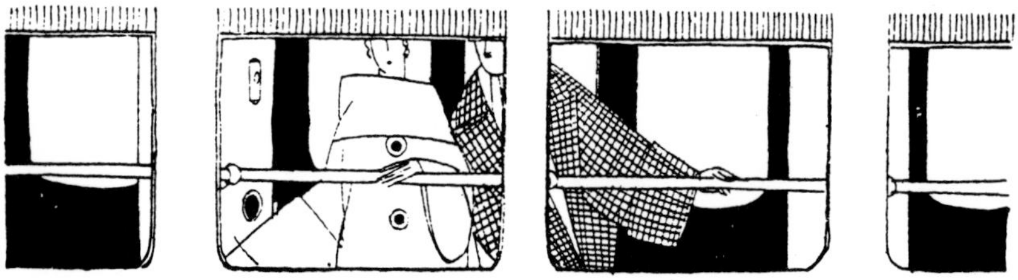

HEALTH

DOCTOR (name, address, phone no, surgery hours) ....

....

....

....

DENTIST (name, address, phone no, surgery hours) ....

....

....

OPTICIAN ....

....

OSTEOPATH ....

....

OTHER LOCAL HEALTH SERVICES ....

....

....

....

....

....

....

....

....

HEALTH: CLINICS

List here details of any clinics attended by members of your family (eg child care, family planning, etc).

CLINIC (name & address)	PHONE NO	SESSION TIMES	PATIENT NO

HEALTH: CLINICS

CLINIC (name & address)	PHONE NO	SESSION TIMES	PATIENT NO

LEISURE

SPORT

List address, phone no, opening hours and any other useful details.

SWIMMING POOL . . . .

. . . .

. . . .

SQUASH COURTS . . . .

. . . .

TENNIS COURTS . . . .

. . . .

SPORTS CENTRE/GYM . . . .

. . . .

GOLF COURSE . . . .

. . . .

KEEP FIT/AEROBICS/YOGA . . . .

. . . .

. . . .

SAILING CLUB . . . .

. . . .

OTHER SPORTS . . . .

. . . .

LEISURE

RECREATION

CINEMAS ....

....

THEATRES ....

....

....

VIDEO HIRE ....

....

LIBRARY (phone no, opening hours) ....

....

....

ADULT EDUCATION CENTRE ....

....

CHILDREN'S EXTRA-CURRICULAR CLASSES (music, ballet etc) ....

....

....

....

OTHER ....

....

....

LEISURE

EATING AND DRINKING

LOCAL RESTAURANTS (phone nos for bookings) . . . .

TAKE-AWAYS (phone nos, delivery details) . . . .

WINE MERCHANT . . . .

IMPORTANT PEOPLE

List here contacts at local organisations to which members of family belong (eg nursery group, Brownies, Scouts, residents' associations etc).

CHURCH, MINISTER, TIMES OF SERVICES

IMPORTANT PEOPLE

NEIGHBOURS AND FRIENDS: address & phone no . . . .

CHILDREN'S FRIENDS: address & phone no . . . .

FAMILY FILE

Fill in the all-important personal particulars for every member of the family. Space is allowed for three adults, so you could include a live-in nanny or grandparent, and four children.

PERSONAL DETAILS (adult)

FULL NAME ....

DATE OF BIRTH ....

WORK ADDRESS, PHONE NO ....

....

....

MEDICAL CARD NO ....

NATIONAL INSURANCE/SOCIAL SECURITY NO ....

PASSPORT NO ....

CLOTHING

WOMEN	MEN
Bust .... Bra size	Chest ....
Waist	Waist ....
Hips	Inside leg ....
Dress size	Collar size ....
Skirt/trouser size	Sock size ....
Shoe size	Shoe size ....
Hat size	Hat size ....
Glove size	Glove size ....

HEALTH DETAILS

BLOOD GROUP ....

CHILDHOOD DISEASES (GIVE ESTIMATED DATE)

CHICKENPOX ....

GERMAN MEASLES ....

GLANDULAR FEVER ....

MEASLES ....

MUMPS ....

WHOOPING COUGH ....

IMMUNISATIONS FOR FOREIGN TRAVEL

Your GP can give you details of which immunisations are needed for which country. Make enquiries well in advance of your travel date.

TYPE	DATE GIVEN	BOOSTER DUE
Cholera		After 6 months:
Hepatitis A		After 3-6 months:
Hepatitis B		After 3-5 years:
Meningitis		Rarely given: consult GP
Polio		After 10 years:
Tetanus		After 10 years:
Typhoid		After 3 years:
Yellow fever *(at certain clinics only)*		After 10 years:

OTHER HEALTH INFORMATION (ALLERGIES, MEDICINES TAKEN, ETC)

....

....

....

....

PERSONAL DETAILS (adult)

FULL NAME ....

DATE OF BIRTH ....

WORK NAME, ADDRESS, PHONE NO ....

....

....

MEDICAL CARD NO ....

NATIONAL INSURANCE/SOCIAL SECURITY NO ....

PASSPORT NO ....

CLOTHING

WOMEN	MEN
Bust .... Bra size	Chest ....
Waist	Waist ....
Hips	Inside leg ....
Dress size	Collar size ....
Skirt/trouser size	Sock size ....
Shoe size	Shoe size ....
Hat size	Hat size ....
Glove size	Glove size ....

HEALTH DETAILS

BLOOD GROUP ....

CHILDHOOD DISEASES (GIVE ESTIMATED DATE)

CHICKENPOX ....

GERMAN MEASLES ....

GLANDULAR FEVER ....

MEASLES ....

MUMPS ....

WHOOPING COUGH ....

IMMUNISATIONS FOR FOREIGN TRAVEL

Your GP can give you details of which immunisations are needed for which country. Make enquiries well in advance of your travel date.

TYPE	DATE GIVEN	BOOSTER DUE
Cholera		After 6 months:
Hepatitis A		After 3-6 months:
Hepatitis B		After 3-5 years:
Meningitis		Rarely given: consult GP
Polio		After 10 years:
Tetanus		After 10 years:
Typhoid		After 3 years:
Yellow fever *(at certain clinics only)*		After 10 years:

OTHER HEALTH INFORMATION (ALLERGIES, MEDICINES TAKEN, ETC)

....

....

....

....

PERSONAL DETAILS (adult)

FULL NAME ....

DATE OF BIRTH ....

WORK NAME, ADDRESS, PHONE NO ....

....

....

MEDICAL CARD NO ....

NATIONAL INSURANCE/SOCIAL SECURITY NO ....

PASSPORT NO ....

CLOTHING

WOMEN

Bust .... Bra size ....

Waist ....

Hips ....

Dress size ....

Skirt/trouser size ....

Shoe size ....

Hat size ....

Glove size ....

MEN

Chest ....

Waist ....

Inside leg ....

Collar size ....

Sock size ....

Shoe size ....

Hat size ....

Glove size ....

HEALTH DETAILS

BLOOD GROUP ....

CHILDHOOD DISEASES (GIVE ESTIMATED DATE)

CHICKENPOX ....

GERMAN MEASLES ....

GLANDULAR FEVER ....

MEASLES ....

MUMPS ....

WHOOPING COUGH ....

IMMUNISATIONS FOR FOREIGN TRAVEL

Your GP can give you details of which immunisations are needed for which country. Make enquiries well in advance of your travel date.

TYPE	DATE GIVEN	BOOSTER DUE
Cholera		After 6 months:
Hepatitis A		After 3-6 months:
Hepatitis B		After 3-5 years:
Meningitis		Rarely given: consult GP
Polio		After 10 years:
Tetanus		After 10 years:
Typhoid		After 3 years:
Yellow fever *(at certain clinics only)*		After 10 years:

OTHER HEALTH INFORMATION (ALLERGIES, MEDICINES TAKEN, ETC)

....

....

....

....

PERSONAL DETAILS (child)

FULL NAME . . . .

DATE OF BIRTH . . . .

NAME, ADDRESS, PHONE NO OF SCHOOL OR COLLEGE . . . .

. . . .

. . . .

HEAD TEACHER. . . . . CLASS TEACHER . . . .

MEDICAL CARD NO . . . .

NATIONAL INSURANCE/SOCIAL SECURITY NO . . . .

PASSPORT NO . . . .

CLOTHING

Height . . . .

Chest . . . .

Waist . . . .

Shoe size . . . .

Hat size . . . .

Glove size . . . .

Other details . . . .

. . . .

. . . .

. . . .

HEALTH DETAILS

BLOOD GROUP ....

DATES OF CONTAGIOUS DISEASES

CHICKENPOX ....

GERMAN MEASLES ....

GLANDULAR FEVER ....

MEASLES ....

MUMPS ....

WHOOPING COUGH ....

DATES OF INNOCULATIONS

TYPE	DATE/S GIVEN	BOOSTER DUE
DPT *(Diphtheria, Whooping Cough, Tetanus)* & Polio		4-5 years of age:
MMR *(Mumps, Measles, Rubella)*		Not needed
BCG (TB)		
Other		

IMMUNISATIONS FOR FOREIGN TRAVEL

Some of these immunisations should not be given to very young children. Your GP can give you details.

TYPE	DATE GIVEN	BOOSTER DUE
Cholera		After 6 months:
Hepatitis A		After 3-6 months:
Hepatitis B		After 3-5 years:
Meningitis		Rarely given: consult GP
Polio		After 10 years:
Tetanus		After 10 years:
Typhoid		After 3 years:
Yellow fever *(at certain clinics only)*		After 10 years:

OTHER HEALTH INFORMATION (ALLERGIES, MEDICINES TAKEN, ETC)

....

....

EDUCATION DETAILS

SCHOOLS/COLLEGES ATTENDED (give dates)

....

....

....

....

....

....

....

EXAMINATIONS

SUBJECT	LEVEL	DATE TAKEN	RESULT (GIVE GRADES)

PERSONAL DETAILS (child)

FULL NAME . . . .

DATE OF BIRTH . . . .

NAME, ADDRESS, PHONE NO OF SCHOOL OR COLLEGE . . . .

. . . .

. . . .

HEAD TEACHER . . . . CLASS TEACHER . . . .

MEDICAL CARD NO . . . .

NATIONAL INSURANCE/SOCIAL SECURITY NO . . . .

PASSPORT NO . . . .

CLOTHING

Height . . . .

Chest . . . .

Waist . . . .

Shoe size . . . .

Hat size . . . .

Glove size . . . .

Other details . . . .

. . . .

. . . .

. . . .

HEALTH DETAILS

BLOOD GROUP ....

DATES OF CONTAGIOUS DISEASES

CHICKENPOX ....

GERMAN MEASLES ....

GLANDULAR FEVER ....

MEASLES ....

MUMPS ....

WHOOPING COUGH ....

DATES OF INNOCULATIONS

TYPE	DATE/S GIVEN	BOOSTER DUE
DPT *(Diphtheria, Whooping Cough, Tetanus)* & Polio		4-5 years of age:
MMR *(Mumps, Measles, Rubella)*		Not needed
BCG (TB)		
Other		

IMMUNISATIONS FOR FOREIGN TRAVEL

Some of these immunisations should not be given to very young children. Your GP can give you details.

TYPE	DATE GIVEN	BOOSTER DUE
Cholera		After 6 months:
Hepatitis A		After 3-6 months:
Hepatitis B		After 3-5 years:
Meningitis		Rarely given: consult GP
Polio		After 10 years:
Tetanus		After 10 years:
Typhoid		After 3 years:
Yellow fever *(at certain clinics only)*		After 10 years:

OTHER HEALTH INFORMATION (ALLERGIES, MEDICINES TAKEN, ETC)

....

....

EDUCATION DETAILS

SCHOOLS/COLLEGES ATTENDED (give dates)

. . . .

. . . .

. . . .

. . . .

. . . .

. . . .

. . . .

EXAMINATIONS

SUBJECT	LEVEL	DATE TAKEN	RESULT (GIVE GRADES)

PERSONAL DETAILS (child)

FULL NAME ....

DATE OF BIRTH ....

NAME, ADDRESS, PHONE NO OF SCHOOL OR COLLEGE ....

....

....

HEAD TEACHER .... CLASS TEACHER ....

MEDICAL CARD NO ....

NATIONAL INSURANCE/SOCIAL SECURITY NO ....

PASSPORT NO ....

CLOTHING

Height ....

Chest ....

Waist ....

Shoe size ....

Hat size ....

Glove size ....

Other details ....

....

....

....

HEALTH DETAILS

BLOOD GROUP ....

DATES OF CONTAGIOUS DISEASES

CHICKENPOX ....

GERMAN MEASLES ....

GLANDULAR FEVER ....

MEASLES ....

MUMPS ....

WHOOPING COUGH ....

DATES OF INNOCULATIONS

TYPE	DATE/S GIVEN	BOOSTER DUE
DPT *(Diphtheria, Whooping Cough, Tetanus)* & Polio		4-5 years of age:
MMR *(Mumps, Measles, Rubella)*		Not needed
BCG (TB)		
Other		

IMMUNISATIONS FOR FOREIGN TRAVEL

Some of these immunisations should not be given to very young children. Your GP can give you details.

TYPE	DATE GIVEN	BOOSTER DUE
Cholera		After 6 months:
Hepatitis A		After 3-6 months:
Hepatitis B		After 3-5 years:
Meningitis		Rarely given: consult GP
Polio		After 10 years:
Tetanus		After 10 years:
Typhoid		After 3 years:
Yellow fever *(at certain clinics only)*		After 10 years:

OTHER HEALTH INFORMATION (ALLERGIES, MEDICINES TAKEN, ETC)

....

....

EDUCATION DETAILS

SCHOOLS/COLLEGES ATTENDED (give dates)

. . . .

. . . .

. . . .

. . . .

. . . .

. . . .

. . . .

EXAMINATIONS

SUBJECT	LEVEL	DATE TAKEN	RESULT (GIVE GRADES)

PERSONAL DETAILS (child)

FULL NAME ....

DATE OF BIRTH ....

NAME, ADDRESS, PHONE NO OF SCHOOL OR COLLEGE ....

....

....

HEAD TEACHER .... CLASS TEACHER ....

MEDICAL CARD NO ....

NATIONAL INSURANCE/SOCIAL SECURITY NO ....

PASSPORT NO ....

CLOTHING

Height ....

Chest ....

Waist ....

Shoe size ....

Hat size ....

Glove size ....

Other details ....

....

....

....

HEALTH DETAILS

BLOOD GROUP ....

DATES OF CONTAGIOUS DISEASES

CHICKENPOX ....

GERMAN MEASLES ....

GLANDULAR FEVER ....

MEASLES ....

MUMPS ....

WHOOPING COUGH ....

DATES OF INNOCULATIONS

TYPE	DATE/S GIVEN	BOOSTER DUE
DPT *(Diphtheria, Whooping Cough, Tetanus)* & Polio		4-5 years of age:
MMR *(Mumps, Measles, Rubella)*		Not needed
BCG (TB)		
Other		

IMMUNISATIONS FOR FOREIGN TRAVEL

Some of these immunisations should not be given to very young children. Your GP can give you details.

TYPE	DATE GIVEN	BOOSTER DUE
Cholera		After 6 months:
Hepatitis A		After 3-6 months:
Hepatitis B		After 3-5 years:
Meningitis		Rarely given: consult GP
Polio		After 10 years:
Tetanus		After 10 years:
Typhoid		After 3 years:
Yellow fever *(at certain clinics only)*		After 10 years:

OTHER HEALTH INFORMATION (ALLERGIES, MEDICINES TAKEN, ETC)

....

....

EDUCATION DETAILS

SCHOOLS/COLLEGES ATTENDED (give dates)

....

....

....

....

....

....

....

EXAMINATIONS

SUBJECT	LEVEL	DATE TAKEN	RESULT (GIVE GRADES)

PETS

DOGS

NAME . . . .

DATE OF BIRTH . . . .

BREED/PEDIGREE DETAILS . . . .

. . . .

. . . .

VACCINATIONS

TYPE	DATE/S GIVEN	BOOSTER DUE
		Annually:
Distemper		
Canine Hepatitis		
Leptospirosis		
Parvovirus		
Rabies		
Other		

VET (name, address, phone no, surgery hours) . . . .

. . . .

. . . .

BOARDING KENNELS (name, address, phone no) . . . .

. . . .

. . . .

NAMES, ADDRESSES, PHONE NOS OF FEEDERS/SITTERS/WALKERS . . . .

. . . .

. . . .

PETS

CATS

NAME ....

DATE OF BIRTH ....

BREED/PEDIGREE DETAILS ....

....

....

VACCINATIONS

TYPE	DATE/S GIVEN	BOOSTER DUE
FIE *(Feline Infectious Enteritis)*		Annually:
FCV *(Feline Calcivirus)*		
FVR *(Feline Viral Rhinotracheitis)*		
Rabies		
Other		

VET (name, address, phone no, surgery hours) ....

....

....

....

BOARDING CATTERY (name, address, phone no) ....

....

....

NAMES, ADDRESSES, PHONE NOS OF FEEDERS/SITTERS ....

....

....

IMPORTANT DATES

Fill in details of family birthdays, anniversaries and special occasions on this month-by-month chart.

JANUARY

....

....

....

....

....

FEBRUARY

....

....

....

....

....

MARCH

....

....

....

....

....

APRIL

....

....

....

....

....

MAY

....

....

....

....

....

JUNE

....

....

....

....

....

IMPORTANT DATES

JULY

AUGUST

SEPTEMBER

OCTOBER

NOVEMBER

DECEMBER

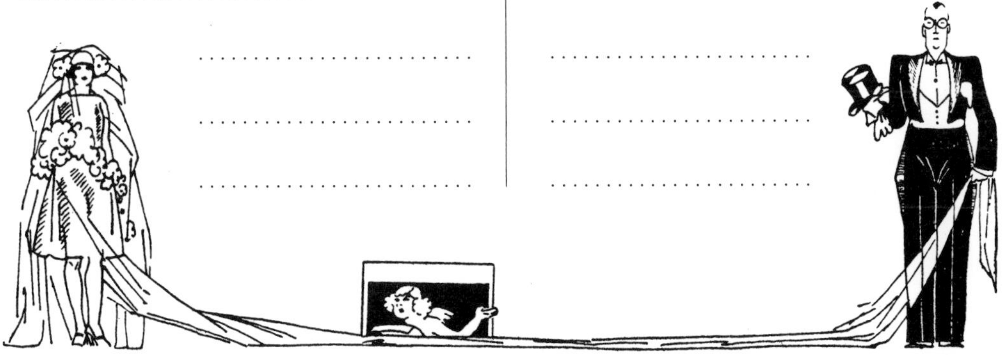

Family Address List

Use this page to jot down the addresses and phone nos of family members whom you contact frequently, or might need to reach quickly.

DOMESTIC LOGBOOK

APPLIANCES

Most domestic appliances periodically need servicing or repair. Keep a record here of important details about appliances and, under 'Servicing and repair history', make a note of who did the work, the date, exactly what was done and the cost.

ITEM. . . . . GUARANTEE EXPIRES . . . .

MAKE AND MODEL NO . . . .
(Serial no. on rating plate)
WHEN AND WHERE BOUGHT . . . .

. . . .

SERVICE CONTRACT . . . .

SERVICE AND REPAIR HISTORY . . . .

. . . .

. . . .

. . . .

ITEM . . . . GUARANTEE EXPIRES . . . .

MAKE AND MODEL NO . . . .
(Serial no. on rating plate)
WHEN AND WHERE BOUGHT . . . .

. . . .

SERVICE CONTRACT . . . .

SERVICE AND REPAIR HISTORY . . . .

. . . .

. . . .

. . . .

APPLIANCES

ITEM.. GUARANTEE EXPIRES ....

MAKE AND MODEL NO ....

(Serial no. on rating plate)

WHEN AND WHERE BOUGHT ....

....

SERVICE CONTRACT ....

SERVICE AND REPAIR HISTORY ....

....

....

....

....

ITEM .... GUARANTEE EXPIRES ....

MAKE AND MODEL NO ....

(Serial no. on rating plate)

WHEN AND WHERE BOUGHT ....

....

SERVICE CONTRACT ....

SERVICE AND REPAIR HISTORY ....

....

....

....

....

APPLIANCES

ITEM. . . . . GUARANTEE EXPIRES . . . .

MAKE AND MODEL NO . . . .
(Serial no. on rating plate)
WHEN AND WHERE BOUGHT . . . .

. . . .

SERVICE CONTRACT . . . .

SERVICE AND REPAIR HISTORY . . . .

. . . .

. . . .

. . . .

. . . .

ITEM . . . . GUARANTEE EXPIRES . . . .

MAKE AND MODEL NO . . . .
(Serial no. on rating plate)
WHEN AND WHERE BOUGHT . . . .

. . . .

SERVICE CONTRACT . . . .

SERVICE AND REPAIR HISTORY . . . .

. . . .

. . . .

. . . .

. . . .

APPLIANCES

ITEM. . . . . GUARANTEE EXPIRES . . . .

MAKE AND MODEL NO . . . .
(Serial no. on rating plate)
WHEN AND WHERE BOUGHT . . . .

. . . .

SERVICE CONTRACT . . . .

SERVICE AND REPAIR HISTORY . . . .

. . . .

. . . .

. . . .

. . . .

ITEM . . . . GUARANTEE EXPIRES . . . .

MAKE AND MODEL NO . . . .
(Serial no. on rating plate)
WHEN AND WHERE BOUGHT . . . .

. . . .

SERVICE CONTRACT . . . .

SERVICE AND REPAIR HISTORY . . . .

. . . .

. . . .

. . . .

. . . .

Appliances

ITEM. . . . . GUARANTEE EXPIRES . . . .

MAKE AND MODEL NO . . . .
(Serial no. on rating plate)
WHEN AND WHERE BOUGHT . . . .

. . . .

SERVICE CONTRACT . . . .

SERVICE AND REPAIR HISTORY . . . .

. . . .

. . . .

. . . .

. . . .

ITEM . . . . GUARANTEE EXPIRES . . . .

MAKE AND MODEL NO . . . .
(Serial no. on rating plate)
WHEN AND WHERE BOUGHT . . . .

. . . .

SERVICE CONTRACT . . . .

SERVICE AND REPAIR HISTORY . . . .

. . . .

. . . .

. . . .

. . . .

APPLIANCES

ITEM. . . . . GUARANTEE EXPIRES . . . .

MAKE AND MODEL NO . . . .

(Serial no. on rating plate)

WHEN AND WHERE BOUGHT . . . .

. . . .

SERVICE CONTRACT . . . .

SERVICE AND REPAIR HISTORY . . . .

. . . .

. . . .

. . . .

. . . .

ITEM . . . . GUARANTEE EXPIRES . . . .

MAKE AND MODEL NO . . . .

(Serial no. on rating plate)

WHEN AND WHERE BOUGHT . . . .

. . . .

SERVICE CONTRACT . . . .

SERVICE AND REPAIR HISTORY . . . .

. . . .

. . . .

. . . .

. . . .

APPLIANCES

ITEM. . . . . GUARANTEE EXPIRES . . . .

MAKE AND MODEL NO . . . .
(Serial no. on rating plate)
WHEN AND WHERE BOUGHT . . . .

. . . .

SERVICE CONTRACT . . . .

SERVICE AND REPAIR HISTORY . . . .

. . . .

. . . .

. . . .

. . . .

ITEM . . . . GUARANTEE EXPIRES . . . .

MAKE AND MODEL NO . . . .
(Serial no. on rating plate)
WHEN AND WHERE BOUGHT . . . .

. . . .

SERVICE CONTRACT . . . .

SERVICE AND REPAIR HISTORY . . . .

. . . .

. . . .

. . . .

. . . .

DOMESTIC ADDRESS LIST

This is the place to keep a record of people such as heating engineers, tv or computer experts, carpet and curtain cleaners, chimney sweeps, locksmiths, etc: anyone, in fact, who repairs, cleans or services any item in the house.

APPLIANCE	NAME OF COMPANY AND CONTACT	ADDRESS AND PHONE NO	COMMENTS

DOMESTIC ADDRESS LIST

APPLIANCE	NAME OF COMPANY AND CONTACT	ADDRESS AND PHONE NO	COMMENTS

HOME IMPROVEMENTS AND REPAIRS

It's easy to forget important details of work done around the house: what it cost to build a new porch; the shade of paint used in the sitting room; all the little extras that crept on to the plumber's last bill. Keep a running record here of any work, large or small, done on your home.

DETAILS OF WORK DONE	DATE	BY WHOM	COST	COMMENTS

HOME IMPROVEMENTS AND REPAIRS

DETAILS OF WORK DONE	DATE	BY WHOM	COST	COMMENTS

Garden Maintenance

From lopping a tree or erecting a shed to repairing a sagging fence – this is the page to record details of all the jobs done in the garden.

Details of Work Done	Date	By Whom	Cost	Comments

GARDEN MAINTENANCE

DETAILS OF WORK DONE	DATE	BY WHOM	COST	COMMENTS

Cars and Drivers

Car 1

MAKE AND MODEL ....

REGISTRATION NO ....

MOT CERTIFICATE EXPIRES .... TAX EXPIRES ....

MILEAGE WHEN PURCHASED ....

NAME, ADDRESS, PHONE NO OF INSUREES ....

....

POLICY NO .... WHO IS COVERED? ....

SERVICING/REPAIR HISTORY ....

....

....

....

....

....

....

....

....

....

....

....

CARS AND DRIVERS

CAR 2

MAKE AND MODEL ....

REGISTRATION NO ....

MOT CERTIFICATE EXPIRES .... TAX EXPIRES ....

MILEAGE WHEN PURCHASED ....

NAME, ADDRESS, PHONE NO OF INSURERS ....

....

POLICY NO .... WHO IS COVERED? ....

SERVICING/REPAIR HISTORY ....

....

....

....

....

....

....

....

CARS AND DRIVERS

DRIVER 1

NAME ....

DRIVING LICENCE ISSUED .... EXPIRES ....

MOTORING ORGANIZATION MEMBERSHIP NO ....

DRIVER 2

NAME ....

DRIVING LICENCE ISSUED .... EXPIRES ....

MOTORING ORGANIZATION MEMBERSHIP NO ....

DRIVER 3

NAME ....

DRIVING LICENCE ISSUED .... EXPIRES ....

MOTORING ORGANIZATION MEMBERSHIP NO ....

WHERE TO GET HELP

NAME, ADDRESS, PHONE NO OF GARAGE ....

....

....

PHONE NO OF MOTORING ORGANIZATION BREAKDOWN SERVICE ....

OTHER DETAILS ....

....

....

KEEP SAFE

Most households have some items that are very attractive to thieves: bicycles, video recorders, cameras, jewellery, paintings. Use these pages to record these items, listing serial numbers where appropriate, and a brief description of each one.

ITEM SERIAL NO/DESCRIPTION

....

....

....

....

....

....

....

....

....

....

....

....

....

....

....

....

....

ITEM	SERIAL NO/DESCRIPTION

ITEM	SERIAL NO/DESCRIPTION

HOUSEHOLD EXPENDITURE

Regular Bills

Use these pages to record details of regular bills, as they are paid. At the end of the year, add up the amounts to give a total which can then be entered on the Annual Budgets, given on pages 76, 77.

GAS	YEAR	YEAR	YEAR	YEAR	YEAR
1ST QUARTER					
2ND QUARTER					
3RD QUARTER					
4TH QUARTER					
TOTAL *(Carry forward to page 76)*					

GAS	YEAR	YEAR	YEAR	YEAR	YEAR
1ST QUARTER					
2ND QUARTER					
3RD QUARTER					
4TH QUARTER					
TOTAL *(Carry forward to page 77)*					

REGULAR BILLS

ELECTRICITY	YEAR	YEAR	YEAR	YEAR	YEAR
1ST QUARTER					
2ND QUARTER					
3RD QUARTER					
4TH QUARTER					
TOTAL *(Carry forward to page 76)*					

ELECTRICITY	YEAR	YEAR	YEAR	YEAR	YEAR
1ST QUARTER					
2ND QUARTER					
3RD QUARTER					
4TH QUARTER					
TOTAL *(Carry forward to page 77)*					

REGULAR BILLS

TELEPHONE	YEAR	YEAR	YEAR	YEAR	YEAR
1ST QUARTER					
2ND QUARTER					
3RD QUARTER					
4TH QUARTER					
TOTAL *(Carry forward to page 76)*					

TELEPHONE	YEAR	YEAR	YEAR	YEAR	YEAR
1ST QUARTER					
2ND QUARTER					
3RD QUARTER					
4TH QUARTER					
TOTAL *(Carry forward to page 77)*					

REGULAR BILLS

COMMUNITY CHARGE *or RATES* *List each family member liable*	YEAR	YEAR	YEAR	YEAR	YEAR
FAMILY TOTAL (Carry forward to page 76)					

COMMUNITY CHARGE *or RATES* *List each family member liable*	YEAR	YEAR	YEAR	YEAR	YEAR
FAMILY TOTAL (Carry forward to page 77)					

REGULAR BILLS

SCHOOL FEES	YEAR	YEAR	YEAR	YEAR	YEAR
1ST TERM					
2ND TERM					
3RD TERM					
TOTAL *(Carry forward to page 76)*					

SCHOOL FEES	YEAR	YEAR	YEAR	YEAR	YEAR
1ST TERM					
2ND TERM					
3RD TERM					
TOTAL *(Carry forward to page 77)*					

OTHER REGULAR PAYMENTS

List all standing orders, direct debits and other regular payments.

YEAR:	AMOUNT	METHOD	FREQUENCY	ANNUAL TOTAL
MORTGAGE/RENT				
INSURANCES				
HP PAYMENTS/LOANS				
MEMBERSHIP FEES				
SEASON TICKET/S				
CAR: TAX INSURANCE MOTORING ORGANIZATION				
HOUSEHOLD HELP				
OTHER				
			GRAND TOTAL	

YEAR:	AMOUNT	METHOD	FREQUENCY	ANNUAL TOTAL
MORTGAGE/RENT				
INSURANCES				
HP PAYMENTS/LOANS				
MEMBERSHIP FEES				
SEASON TICKET/S				
CAR: TAX INSURANCE MOTORING ORGANIZATION				
HOUSEHOLD HELP				
OTHER				
			GRAND TOTAL	

Other Regular Payments

YEAR:	AMOUNT	METHOD	FREQUENCY	ANNUAL TOTAL
MORTGAGE/RENT				
INSURANCES				
HP PAYMENTS/LOANS				
MEMBERSHIP FEES				
SEASON TICKET/S				
CAR: TAX INSURANCE MOTORING ORGANIZATION				
HOUSEHOLD HELP				
OTHER				
			GRAND TOTAL	

YEAR:	AMOUNT	METHOD	FREQUENCY	ANNUAL TOTAL
MORTGAGE/RENT				
INSURANCES				
HP PAYMENTS/LOANS				
MEMBERSHIP FEES				
SEASON TICKET/S				
CAR: TAX INSURANCE MOTORING ORGANIZATION				
HOUSEHOLD HELP				
OTHER				
			GRAND TOTAL	

OTHER REGULAR PAYMENTS

YEAR:	AMOUNT	METHOD	FREQUENCY	ANNUAL TOTAL
MORTGAGE/RENT				
INSURANCES				
HP PAYMENTS/LOANS				
MEMBERSHIP FEES				
SEASON TICKET/S				
CAR: TAX INSURANCE MOTORING ORGANIZATION				
HOUSEHOLD HELP				
OTHER				
			GRAND TOTAL	

YEAR:	AMOUNT	METHOD	FREQUENCY	ANNUAL TOTAL
MORTGAGE/RENT				
INSURANCES				
HP PAYMENTS/LOANS				
MEMBERSHIP FEES				
SEASON TICKET/S				
CAR: TAX INSURANCE MOTORING ORGANIZATION				
HOUSEHOLD HELP				
OTHER				
			GRAND TOTAL	

OTHER REGULAR PAYMENTS

YEAR:	AMOUNT	METHOD	FREQUENCY	ANNUAL TOTAL
MORTGAGE/RENT				
INSURANCES				
HP PAYMENTS/LOANS				
MEMBERSHIP FEES				
SEASON TICKET/S				
CAR: TAX INSURANCE MOTORING ORGANIZATION				
HOUSEHOLD HELP				
OTHER				
			GRAND TOTAL	

YEAR:	AMOUNT	METHOD	FREQUENCY	ANNUAL TOTAL
MORTGAGE/RENT				
INSURANCES				
HP PAYMENTS/LOANS				
MEMBERSHIP FEES				
SEASON TICKET/S				
CAR: TAX INSURANCE MOTORING ORGANIZATION				
HOUSEHOLD HELP				
OTHER				
			GRAND TOTAL	

OTHER REGULAR PAYMENTS

YEAR:	AMOUNT	METHOD	FREQUENCY	ANNUAL TOTAL
MORTGAGE/RENT				
INSURANCES				
HP PAYMENTS/LOANS				
MEMBERSHIP FEES				
SEASON TICKET/S				
CAR: TAX INSURANCE MOTORING ORGANIZATION				
HOUSEHOLD HELP				
OTHER				
			GRAND TOTAL	

YEAR:	AMOUNT	METHOD	FREQUENCY	ANNUAL TOTAL
MORTGAGE/RENT				
INSURANCES				
HP PAYMENTS/LOANS				
MEMBERSHIP FEES				
SEASON TICKET/S				
CAR: TAX INSURANCE MOTORING ORGANIZATION				
HOUSEHOLD HELP				
OTHER				
			GRAND TOTAL	

ANNUAL BUDGETS

Enter the yearly grand totals from from the preceding pages here, to give an overall picture of your annual expenditure on major items. The information can be used to help budget for major expenses in the year ahead, and will also build up into a useful year-by-year comparison.

ANNUAL TOTALS	YEAR	YEAR	YEAR	YEAR	YEAR
GAS					
ELECTRICITY					
TELEPHONE					
COMMUNITY CHARGE OR RATES					
SCHOOL FEES					
WATER RATES					
OTHER REGULAR PAYMENTS					
TOTAL FOR YEAR					

Annual Budgets

Annual Totals	Year	Year	Year	Year	Year
Gas					
Electricity					
Telephone					
Community Charge or Rates					
School Fees					
Water Rates					
Other Regular Payments					
Total for Year					

ANNUAL REMINDERS

When planning your budget at the beginning of the year, use this checklist to remind you when irregular or one-off payments and other expenses, such as holidays and family celebrations, are likely to fall. Note too, under each month, any standing orders and direct debits which are paid at odd intervals during the year, so that you can bear them in mind when planning the rest of the month's expenditure.

MONTH	ITEMS	AMOUNT
JANUARY		
FEBRUARY		
MARCH		
APRIL		

ANNUAL REMINDERS

MONTH	ITEMS	AMOUNT
MAY		
JUNE		
JULY		
AUGUST		

Annual Reminders

Month	Items	Amount
September		
October		
November		
December		

FINANCE

MORTGAGE

Information about your mortgage loan should be entered here. Don't forget to enter the monthly repayments under Other Regular Payments, pages 71-75.

NAME, ADDRESS, PHONE NO OF BUILDING SOCIETY/BANK ....

....

MORTGAGE ACCOUNT NO ....

IN WHOSE NAME? ....

AMOUNT OF LOAN ....

TYPE OF MORTGAGE ....

DATE TAKEN OUT .... TERM ....

MONTHLY REPAYMENT ....

SECOND MORTGAGE

NAME, ADDRESS, PHONE NO OF BUILDING SOCIETY/BANK ....

....

MORTGAGE ACCOUNT NO ....

IN WHOSE NAME? ....

AMOUNT OF LOAN ....

TYPE OF MORTGAGE ....

DATE TAKEN OUT .... TERM ....

MONTHLY REPAYMENT ....

PENSIONS

Enter information about personal pension schemes here. Don't forget to enter the monthly premium under Other Regular Payments, pages 71-75, as well.

NAME, ADDRESS, PHONE NO OF PENSION COMPANY ....

....

....

POLICY NO ....

IN WHOSE NAME? ....

AGE WHEN PENSION BEGINS ....

BENEFITS PROVIDED ....

MONTHLY PREMIUM ....

....

....

....

....

Charge/Credit Card Record

Make a list of every plastic card you own – credit cards, charge cards, cheque guarantee cards, cash cards etc – and add the phone no to ring if a card is lost or stolen. Do not *list PIN numbers.*

TYPE OF CARD	NO	WHO TO RING

INSURANCE

PROPERTY AND BELONGINGS

List here details of all insurance policies which relate to your home and any properties you own, and the contents. Don't forget to list the premiums under Other Regular Payments, on pages 71-75.

NAME, ADDRESS, PHONE NO OF INSURERS ....

....

....

POLICY NO ....

DETAILS OF COVER..

....

....

....

PREMIUM: AMOUNT AND FREQUENCY ....

NAME, ADDRESS, PHONE NO OF INSURERS ....

....

....

POLICY NO ....

DETAILS OF COVER..

....

....

....

PREMIUM: AMOUNT AND FREQUENCY ....

PROPERTY AND BELONGINGS

NAME, ADDRESS, PHONE NO OF INSURERS . . . .

. . . .

. . . .

POLICY NO . . . .

DETAILS OF COVER. . . . .

. . . .

. . . .

. . . .

PREMIUM: AMOUNT AND FREQUENCY . . . .

NAME, ADDRESS, PHONE NO OF INSURERS . . . .

. . . .

. . . .

POLICY NO . . . .

DETAILS OF COVER. . . . .

. . . .

. . . .

. . . .

PREMIUM: AMOUNT AND FREQUENCY . . . .

Property and Belongings

NAME, ADDRESS, PHONE NO OF INSURERS ....

....

....

POLICY NO ....

DETAILS OF COVER..

....

....

....

PREMIUM: AMOUNT AND FREQUENCY ....

NAME, ADDRESS, PHONE NO OF INSURERS ....

....

....

POLICY NO ....

DETAILS OF COVER..

....

....

....

PREMIUM: AMOUNT AND FREQUENCY ....

LIFE AND HEALTH

List here details of any life policies you hold, plus any which cover you for illness or disability. Remember to enter premiums under Other Regular Payments, pages 71-75.

NAME, ADDRESS, PHONE NO OF INSURERS ....

....

....

POLICY NO ....

DETAILS OF COVER..

....

....

WITH/WITHOUT PROFITS .... EXPIRY DATE ....

PREMIUM: AMOUNT AND FREQUENCY ....

NAME, ADDRESS, PHONE NO OF INSURERS

....

....

POLICY NO ....

DETAILS OF COVER.....................

....

....

WITH/WITHOUT PROFITS .... EXPIRY DATE ....

PREMIUM: AMOUNT AND FREQUENCY ....

LIFE AND HEALTH

NAME, ADDRESS, PHONE NO OF INSURERS ....

....

....

POLICY NO ....

DETAILS OF COVER..

....

....

WITH/WITHOUT PROFITS .... EXPIRY DATE ....

PREMIUM: AMOUNT AND FREQUENCY ....

NAME, ADDRESS, PHONE NO OF INSURERS ....

....

....

POLICY NO ....

DETAILS OF COVER..

....

....

WITH/WITHOUT PROFITS .... EXPIRY DATE ....

PREMIUM: AMOUNT AND FREQUENCY ....

LIFE AND HEALTH

NAME, ADDRESS, PHONE NO OF INSURERS ....

....

....

POLICY NO ....

DETAILS OF COVER...

....

....

WITH/WITHOUT PROFITS .... EXPIRY DATE ....

PREMIUM: AMOUNT AND FREQUENCY ....

NAME, ADDRESS, PHONE NO OF INSURERS ....

....

....

POLICY NO ....

DETAILS OF COVER...

....

....

WITH/WITHOUT PROFITS .... EXPIRY DATE ....

PREMIUM: AMOUNT AND FREQUENCY ....

OTHER INSURANCE

Use this page to list details of any other insurance policies you hold. Don't forget small items, such as contact lens cover. Details of car insurance/s are on pages 59, 60 and 71-75, but you may wish to list them again here.

NAME, ADDRESS, PHONE NO OF INSURERS	POLICY NO	DETAILS OF COVER AND RENEWAL DATE	PREMIUM: AMOUNT AND FREQUENCY

WHERE TO FIND . . .

WHERE TO FIND . . .

Tell anyone who might need access to important items or documents in a hurry, that their whereabouts are listed here – and make sure that everything remains in its designated home!

THE FAMILY

WILL/S (give address of bank or solicitor/lawyer, and names and addresses of executors). . . . .

. . . .

. . . .

. . . .

PASSPORT/S . . . .

BIRTH CERTIFICATES . . . .

MARRIAGE CERTIFICATE . . . .

EXAMINATION CERTIFICATES . . . .

OTHER . . . .

THE HOME

DEEDS OF HOUSE (if not lodged with Building Soc) . . . .

. . . .

MORTGAGE DOCUMENTS . . . .

ANY OTHER DEEDS OR PROPERTY DOCUMENTS (specify) . . . .

. . . .

SPARE HOUSE KEYS . . . .

TV LICENCE . . . .

OTHER . . . .

WHERE TO FIND . . .

FINANCIAL

BUILDING SOCIETY PASS BOOK/S . . . .

. . . .

SAVINGS CERTIFICATES, PREMIUM BONDS . . . .

. . . .

SHARE CERTIFICATES . . . .

COPIES OF INCOME TAX RETURNS . . . .

PENSION DOCUMENTS . . . .

OTHER . . . .

. . . .

INSURANCE POLICIES

LIST EACH POLICY SEPARATELY, WITH ITS WHEREABOUTS.

. . . .

. . . .

. . . .

. . . .

. . . .

. . . .

. . . .

. . . .

WHERE TO FIND . . .

CARS

List details separately for each car you own.

CAR 1 (specify make and registration no) . . . .

INSURANCE POLICY . . . .

MOT CERTIFICATE . . . .

VEHICLE REGISTRATION DOCUMENT . . . .

OWNER'S HANDBOOK . . . .

SPARE KEYS . . . .

CAR 2 (specify make and registration no) . . . .

INSURANCE POLICY . . . .

MOT CERTIFICATE . . . .

VEHICLE REGISTRATION DOCUMENT . . . .

OWNER'S HANDBOOK . . . .

SPARE KEYS . . . .

DRIVING LICENCE/S . . . .

. . . .

. . . .

. . . .

. . . .